This Book Belongs to

Randall P. Van Ordt

August 13, 2006

BIBLE STORIES

A TREASURY FOR YOUNG READERS

Illustrated by
SIMONE BONI
FRANCESCA D'OTTAVI
PAOLA RAVAGLIA

Retold by
JANE PARKER RESNICK

COURAGE
BOOKS
AN IMPRINT OF RUNNING PRESS
PHILADELPHIA • LONDON

Canadian representatives: General Publishing Co., Ltd., 30 Lesmill Road, Don Mills, Ontario M3B 2T6.

9 8 7 6 5 4 3 2 1
Digit on right indicates the number of this printing.

Library of Congress Cataloging-in-Publication Number 94–72598

ISBN 1–56138–485–2

The art in this book was supplied by McRae Books, Borgo Ognissanti, 62–50123 Florence, Italy.
Jacket design by Toby Schmidt
Typography: Trump Mediaeval by Richard Conklin
Printed and bound in Hong Kong

Published by Courage Books, an imprint of
Running Press Book Publishers
125 South Twenty-second Street
Philadelphia, Pennsylvania 19103–4399

CONTENTS

THE CREATION

In the beginning God created the heavens and the earth. There was a great, dark emptiness filled only with the spirit of God.

And God said, "Let there be light." And there was light. And God saw that the light was good. God separated the light from darkness and He called the light Day and the dark Night. And the morning and the evening were the first day.

On the second day, God said, "Let there be sky over all the world, and let it be called Heaven." God made the clouds and placed them high above the waters. And God saw that it was good.

On the third day, God said, "Let the waters under the heavens be gathered together and let the dry land appear." God created mountains and valleys, plains and deserts. He called the dry land Earth and He called the waters Seas. And God said, "Let the earth bring forth grass and herbs, flowers and trees." And it was so. He created plants, each with its own seed, so that the earth would bloom forever. And God saw that it was good.

On the fourth day, God said, "Let there be lights in the heavens to separate the day from the night." God made the sun and moon and stars to give light upon the earth and to mark the seasons and the years. He made the sun to rule the day and the moon to rule the night. And God saw that it was good.

On the fifth day, God said, "Let the waters bring forth living creatures and let birds fly in the heavens above the earth." God created great whales and tiny fish and every creature that moves in the seas. And God created the mighty eagle and the delicate sparrow and every bird that flies in the heavens. And the earth was no longer silent. And God saw

that it was good. On the
sixth day, God said, "Let the
earth bring forth living creatures, cattle and beasts and creeping
things." God made the cattle and horses, snakes and lizards, wolves and
rabbits, and all the creatures that live on land. And God saw that it was good.

And God said, "Let us make man in our image, after our likeness. And let him
have rule over the fish of the sea, over the birds of the air, over the cattle and beasts,
and over all the earth."

And so God created man in his own image. He made man of dust from the
ground and breathed life into his nostrils. God called man Adam. And God said,
"Behold, I have given you rule over every fish in the sea and every creature that
walks upon the earth and you shall name them." And Adam did.

Then God said, "It is not good for man to be alone." God caused a deep sleep to
fall upon Adam, and while he slept, God took one of his ribs and closed up the flesh
in its place. From Adam's rib, God made a woman. And she was named Eve.

When the heavens and the earth were finished, and all living creatures were upon
the land, God saw everything that He had created, and it was good.

On the seventh day, God rested. And He blessed the seventh day and made it
holy, because on that day God rested from all the work of Creation.

NOAH'S ARK

Noah was an old man when God spoke to him. The children of Adam and Eve and their children and their children's children had spread over the earth. But people had forgotten God and His teachings. They acted in evil ways and were not good to one another. God saw their wickedness, and His heart was torn.

So the Lord said: "I will make an end to all violence and evil. I will destroy man, whom I created, and the beasts of the earth and the birds of the air, for I am sorry that I made them."

But Noah found favor in the eyes of the Lord. Noah was a righteous man, and he and his wife had three sons who were also good men: Shem, Ham, and Japheth.

So God spoke to Noah: "Build an ark," He commanded. "Make it of gopher wood. Cover it with pitch to keep out the water. Erect three levels and a roof. Make the ark 45 feet high, 450 feet long, and 75 feet wide."

Noah listened in wonder. An ark! But why? And the Lord said, "Behold! I shall bring a flood

and everything upon the earth shall die. But you Noah, I will save, for I have seen that you are a righteous man. Your wife and your sons and your sons' wives shall enter the ark with you. And you shall take two of every living thing, male and female, two of every beast of the earth, every creeping thing, and every bird of the air. And you shall gather every kind of food for you and the animals."

Noah did what God commanded because he believed in the Lord. He built an ark on dry land. His sons gathered the animals and collected the food. Everyone who heard of Noah and his ark laughed, for they no longer believed in God, and they could not imagine a flood that would destroy everything.

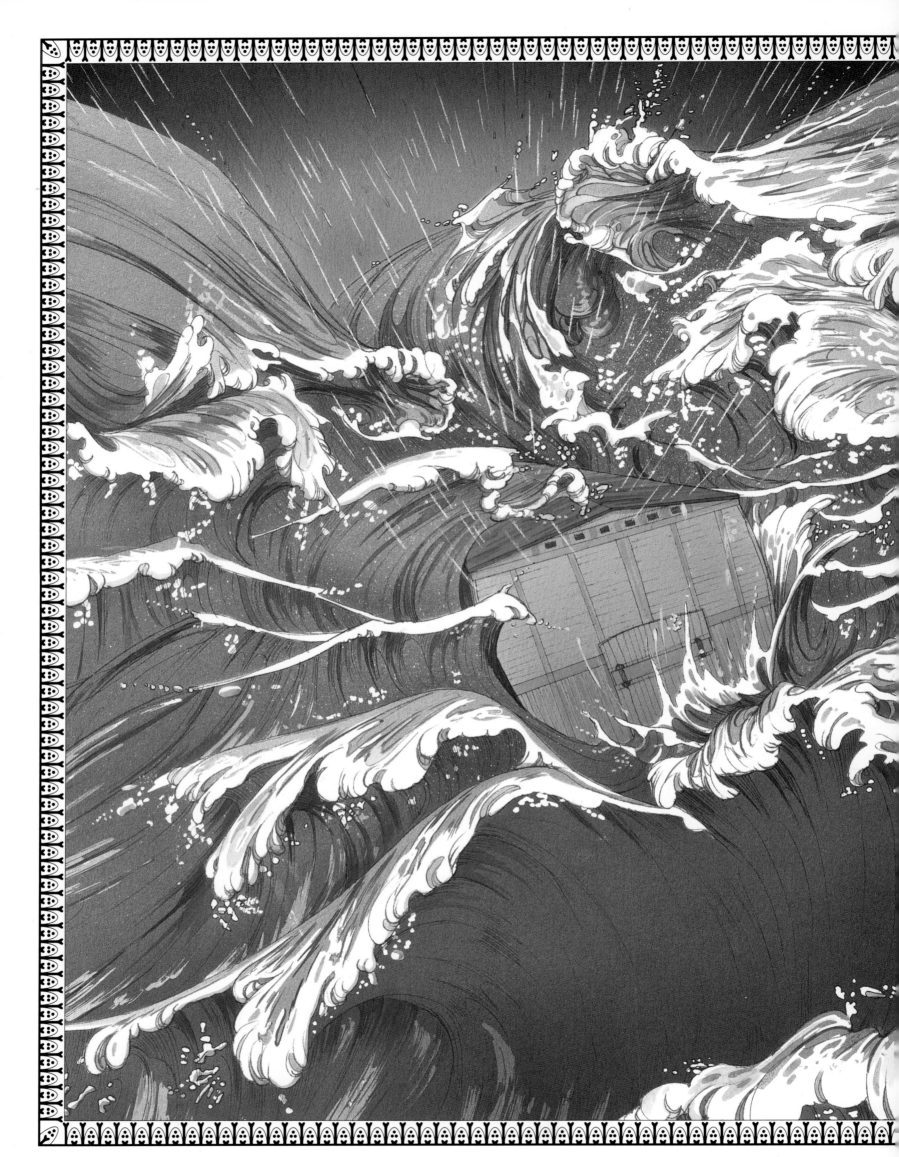

The time came when God told Noah to enter the ark. "It will rain for forty days and forty nights," said the Lord. "Take your wife and your sons and your sons' wives and two of every living thing with you into the ark, for whatever is left on land will be washed from the face of the earth."

So Noah and his family and all the birds and beasts entered the ark, male and female, two by two. After seven days, the windows of the heavens opened, and rain began to fall upon the earth. It rained for forty days and forty nights. Rivers and streams rose to cover the ground. Water climbed over the hills and covered the mountains. The whole world was water. Noah's ark floated alone on the rising flood. The ark drifted on a vast sea, holding the only life on earth.

At the end of forty days and forty nights, the rains stopped. And God remembered Noah. He caused a wind to blow over the earth, and the waters began slowly to go down. For a hundred and fifty days, the ark bobbed in the water with no land in sight. Until, at last, the water fell below the mountain peaks and Noah's ark came to rest upon the mountain of Ararat. Still, no land could be seen. At the end of forty more days, Noah opened the window of the ark and sent a dove into the cool air. He knew the dove would find land, if there were any land to be found. But the dove found no resting place, and soon returned.

Seven days later, Noah again sent the dove into the open air. That evening, she returned with the leaf of an olive tree in her beak. Then Noah knew that the tops of trees had raised their heads above the waters. Seven days later, he released the dove again. This time, she did not return. Water no longer covered the earth.

And God spoke to Noah again: "Go out of the ark and take with you your wife and your sons and your sons' wives and every living thing, beasts and birds and creeping things, so that they may breed and multiply upon the earth."

And two by two, every living thing left the ark with Noah and his family. The world was alive again.

Then Noah built an altar of thanksgiving to the Lord. God was pleased with what He saw in Noah's heart, and He blessed Noah and his family.

God spread a rainbow of glorious colors across the sky, and said, "This rainbow is a sign of my promise. Never again will a flood wash the living creatures from the earth."

JOSEPH'S COAT

 Joseph had a beautiful coat of many colors. His father, Jacob, gave it to him because he loved the boy so much. But Joseph's ten older brothers, who were rough grown men, were jealous and hated Joseph. His younger brother, Benjamin, was then a child.

When Joseph was seventeen, he had a dream. "Listen to my dream," he said to his brothers. "We were in the fields making tall bundles of wheat. My bundle stood up and all of yours bowed down to it."

"Ha!" one brother said angrily. "So you think you will be our ruler?"

Then Joseph had another dream. "In my dream I saw the sun and moon and eleven stars bowing down to me."

Even his father was upset by this dream. "Does this mean your mother and I and your brothers will bow down to you?" he demanded.

Yet Jacob wondered if the dream might be true. Joseph's brothers did, too, and they hated Joseph even more.

The men in Jacob's family were shepherds and they traveled far in search of pastures for their sheep. Once, Jacob's ten older sons were away for a long time and he began to worry. He sent Joseph to find them.

After many difficult hours, Joseph came to a place where he could see his brothers in the distance. They saw him, too, coming toward them in his coat of many colors that they hated so much. Their hearts clenched with jealousy.

"Let us kill him and throw him into a pit," they said.

When Joseph reached his brothers, they stripped him of his coat and cast him into a deep pit without food or water. As Joseph cried for help, his brothers spied a caravan of merchants heading across the desert, and one brother had an idea.

"Why must we kill Joseph?" he asked. "The Ishmaelites are on their way to Egypt. We can sell him to these merchants." And so they sold their brother to the Ishmaelites.

Then they killed a goat and dipped Joseph's coat in the blood. When their father, Jacob, saw the once-beautiful coat so terribly stained he cried out, "Some wild beast has eaten my son Joseph." And he ripped his clothes in grief and would not be comforted by anyone, not even Benjamin, whom he loved almost as much as Joseph.

The older brothers said nothing of what they knew.

Even in slavery, the Lord was with Joseph. The man who bought Joseph was named Potiphar. He served the King of Egypt, the Pharaoh, as the captain of his guard. Potiphar was a good man. He quickly recognized that Joseph was no ordinary slave and, after a while, he put him in charge of all his household.

Joseph was not unhappy there, and he grew into a fine young man. But trouble brewed in the household. Potiphar's wife accused Joseph of a crime, and even though he was innocent, he was sent to prison.

Joseph was in the Pharaoh's own prison, and even there God was with him. The Pharaoh's chief butler and chief baker were also there because they had offended the Pharaoh.

One night these two men had dreams that puzzled them. In Pharaoh's court, dreams were taken seriously as ways to tell the future, and there were wise men who understood them. The two men were unhappy because there was no one in prison to help them with the meaning of their dreams. They told Joseph.

And Joseph said, "Do not the meanings of dreams belong to God? Am I not God's servant? Tell me your dreams."

The butler said, "I dreamed of three branches with buds on them. The buds blossomed into grapes, and I squeezed the grapes into Pharaoh's cup."

And Joseph said, "In three days you will return to serve Pharaoh as you did before." Then Joseph added, "I beg you to ask Pharaoh to free me, for I have done nothing wrong." The butler promised.

Then the baker said, "I dreamed there were three baskets on my head, one above the other. In the top basket were baked foods for Pharaoh. Birds flew down and ate the food. What does it mean?"

Joseph did not like what he had to say: "In three days, Pharaoh will hang you from a tree. And birds will eat your flesh."

Three days later, the butler was released, and he returned to Pharaoh's table. The baker was hanged, as Joseph said he would be.

In his joy, the butler did not remember his promise to Joseph.

Two years passed. One night the King of Egypt dreamed one strange dream and then another. He was troubled by them and sent for all the wise men in Egypt, but

none could tell him the meaning of his dreams. Then the chief butler remembered Joseph, and Pharaoh sent for him at once.

The King was surprised to see a Hebrew from Canaan. "I have been told that you understand the meaning of dreams," he said to Joseph.

"The understanding is not mine, but God's," Joseph answered. "The Lord will give me the answer for you."

So Pharaoh told Joseph his dreams: "I saw seven fat and healthy cows come out of a river and go to graze on a grassy meadow. Then seven ugly, bony cows came up and ate the fat ones. But the thin cows remained as scrawny as before.

"Then I dreamed that I saw a stalk of corn with seven good, full ears on it. Then seven shrunken, wilted ears sprang up and ate the seven good ears, and I woke up!" Pharaoh said.

"It is one dream," Joseph said. "God is showing Pharaoh what is going to happen. The seven fat cows and seven good ears of corn are seven years of rich harvests and plenty. The seven lean cows and seven shrunken ears are the next seven years of no rainfall, poor harvests and no food."

Then Joseph went on, "God is sending Pharaoh a warning so that he may prepare for the bad years that will follow the good. Let Pharaoh choose a man who can buy grain and store it, honestly and justly, during the rich harvests, so that there will be food when the famine begins."

The great King sat in silent thought. Then he said, "Who would be better than the man God has shown all this? You, Joseph, shall be in charge. My people shall be ruled by your word. Only I, Pharaoh, shall be above you." Then Pharaoh gave Joseph the ring he wore on his own finger and proclaimed, "Behold, I have set you over all of Egypt!"

Joseph was thirty years old when he took command of Egypt's grain. He married and had two children. He completed his task well and was respected throughout the land. During the seven years of plenty, he gathered a store of grain in every city in

Egypt. When the seven years without food came, famine spread over all of Egypt and the surrounding lands. Only Egypt had food, so people came to buy grain from Joseph.

Famine spread to the land of Canaan, where Jacob and his family still lived. And Jacob said to his sons, "Go to Egypt, for soon we will have no food for our children." But Jacob kept his youngest son, Benjamin, home.

Joseph's ten older brothers came to Egypt and, like everyone else seeking grain, they bowed down before him. But they did not recognize him.

Joseph knew them at once. He held nothing against them, but he wanted to see if they were still harsh and cruel men.

"You are spies!" he said roughly.

"No," Reuben, the oldest, answered. "We are ten of the sons of Jacob of Canaan. Our youngest brother stays with our father and one brother has been lost to us."

"I say you are spies!" Joseph insisted. "You will not leave here until I see this younger brother," he demanded, for he longed to see Benjamin.

"To prove to me that you are not spies and that I should not kill you," Joseph said, "leave one of you here in prison. Take food, go back to Canaan, and return with your brother Benjamin, and you shall all be free."

The brothers had no choice. One brother, Simeon, was kept behind. The others returned to Canaan. When they told Jacob what had happened, he refused to let Benjamin go. But time passed and the family was again without food.

And so the brothers took Benjamin and returned to Egypt. When they bowed before Joseph, he saw Benjamin, and he was overcome with joy. But Joseph was not yet ready to reveal himself. He was not a cruel man, but he wanted to see that his brothers had really changed. He put them to one last test.

Joseph released Simeon as he had promised and then had his brothers' sacks filled with grain. But he ordered his men to put his silver drinking cup into Benjamin's sack. The brothers left without knowing what they carried.

They had not gone far when Joseph sent his guards after them. The soldiers accused the brothers of taking Joseph's silver cup.

"We are not thieves!" the brothers protested.

But when the sacks were searched, the silver cup was found in Benjamin's bag.

Benjamin was taken prisoner. The others were free to go, but instead, they returned with Benjamin, to protect him.

When Joseph saw that the brothers did not leave Benjamin alone to take the blame, he was happy. Still, he received them with a stern face.

Judah, the brother who had been most cruel to Joseph, approached him. "We did not take the cup," Judah began. "We do not know what happened, but we believe God is punishing us. If one of us is guilty, then all of us are guilty. Let us all stay as your slaves."

"No!" Joseph answered. "Only the man with the silver cup must remain with me." Now, he thought, is their chance to escape and leave Benjamin behind.

But they did not. Judah came forward again. "If we return without Benjamin," he said, "our father, Jacob, will surely die of sorrow. Since the death of our brother, Joseph, the boy is everything to him. I promised that Benjamin would return. Please," he begged, "let me stay in his place, for I could not bear my father's sadness if his youngest son is not returned."

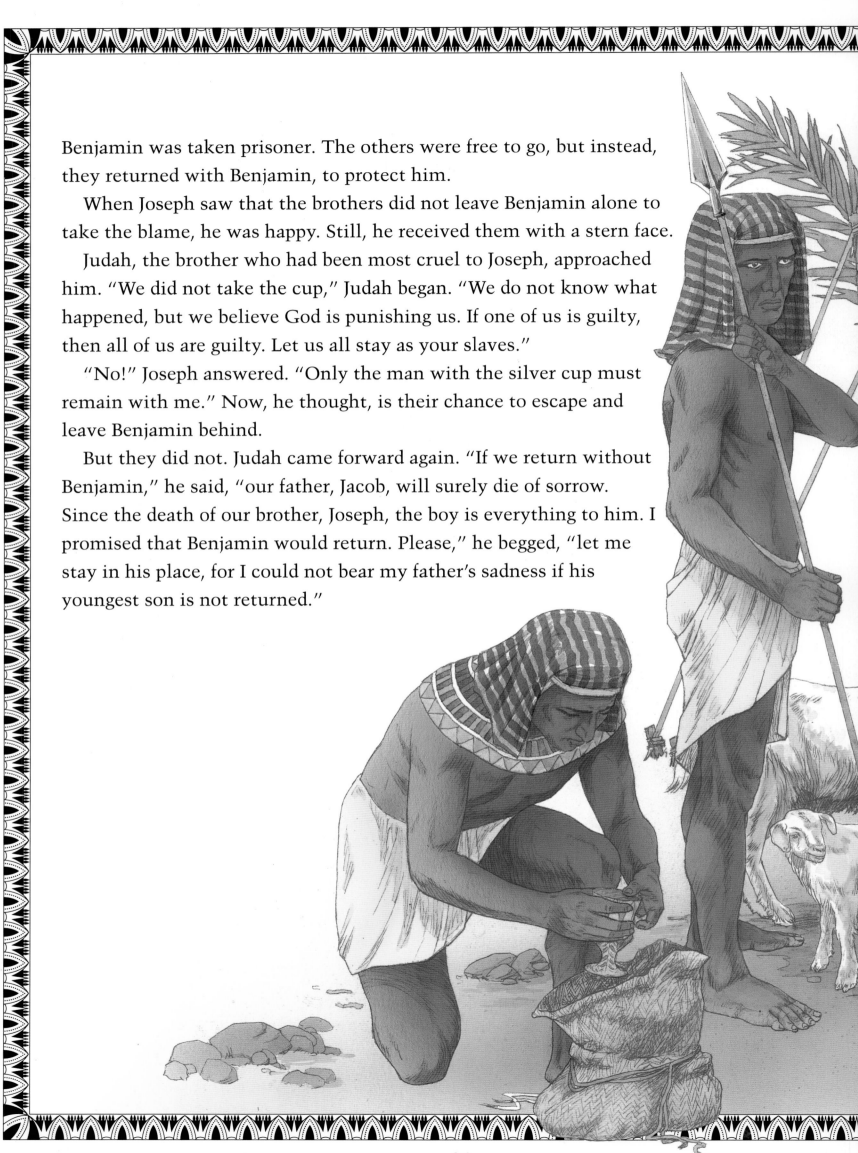

Joseph knew, then, that his brothers had truly changed, and he could keep silent no longer. "I am your brother Joseph whom you sold into Egypt!" he cried out. And he embraced Benjamin with joy and all his other brothers, too.

The brothers cried in disbelief and were afraid, but Joseph said, "Do not be angry with yourselves for selling me, for God has sent me here to save our people's lives. Hurry now and bring our father here to me."

When Jacob heard that his son Joseph was alive and governor over the land of Egypt, he wept with happiness.

Jacob and his family came to Egypt, and Pharaoh welcomed them as the people of Joseph, trusted servant of the King.

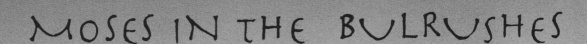

MOSES IN THE BULRUSHES

The children of Israel who came after Joseph and his brothers lived in Egypt for hundreds of years. Their families grew and they lived peacefully among the Egyptians.

But a Pharaoh came to power who feared people from other lands. He was afraid the Hebrews would become mightier than the Egyptians and rise up against them.

So Pharaoh thought: "I shall make their lives hard." And he commanded: "The Hebrews shall be slaves."

Pharaoh set slave drivers over the Hebrew people and made them work harder than men ever worked before. But they did not weaken. Instead, the people of Israel grew stronger still.

Finally, Pharaoh found a way to destroy their strength.

This was Pharaoh's command: "Every son that is born to the Israelites shall be cast into the river Nile."

Now there was a Hebrew woman named Jochebed. She and her husband had two children, Aaron and Miriam. After the Pharaoh's terrible word became law, Jochebed had another child—a boy. Even though Pharaoh's guards were everywhere, searching for boy babies, Jochebed was able to keep her son hidden for three months.

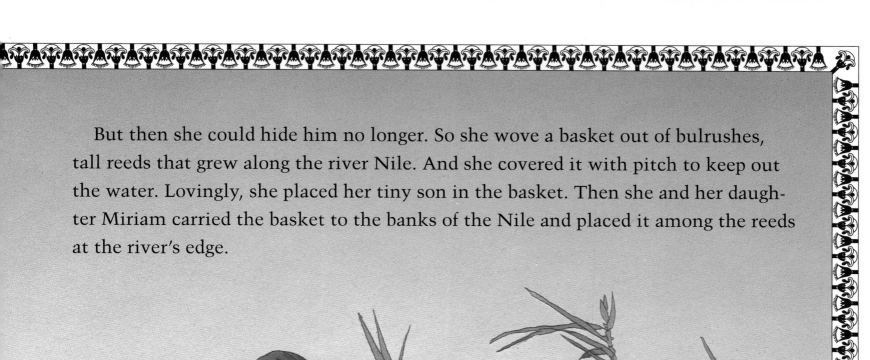

But then she could hide him no longer. So she wove a basket out of bulrushes, tall reeds that grew along the river Nile. And she covered it with pitch to keep out the water. Lovingly, she placed her tiny son in the basket. Then she and her daughter Miriam carried the basket to the banks of the Nile and placed it among the reeds at the river's edge.

Jochebed left in sorrow. But Miriam stayed behind, hiding among the tall reeds to see what would become of her little brother.

A group of women came into view. They wore fine clothes and spoke in gentle voices. They were maidens bringing the Princess, Pharaoh's daughter, to the river to bathe. As Miriam watched from her hiding place, the women walked to the edge of the Nile. Suddenly, the Princess saw the little basket. At once, she sent a maid to bring it to her.

When she opened the basket, the baby began to cry. Miriam held her breath. Then she saw the Princess smile and gently lift the baby. "This is one of the Hebrew children," she said. And she could not think of letting this innocent baby die.

Bravely, Miriam approached the Princess. "Shall I call a nurse to care for the child?" she asked, for it was the custom for wealthy Egyptian women to have nurses for their babies.

"Yes, go," Pharaoh's daughter said to her.

Miriam rushed to find her mother. Jochebed came and saw the Princess holding the baby.

"Will you take this child and nurse him for me?" Pharaoh's daughter asked softly.

With a glad heart, Jochebed took her son home to give him a mother's true love and care. She no longer had to fear for his life, for he was to be the child of Pharaoh's daughter.

When the boy was old enough to leave his mother, Jochebed took him to the Princess. Pharaoh's daughter named him Moses, which means "to draw out," because, she said, "I drew him out of the water." And Moses was raised in the court of Egypt to be an Egyptian prince.

DAVID AND GOLIATH

David was a mighty King of Israel. But when he was a boy, he was a shepherd. He lived in Bethlehem with his father and seven older brothers. David was a fine young man. He could play the harp so sweetly that his music brought peace to troubled souls. He was also a good shepherd. Alone with the flocks, he carried a tall walking stick called a staff, a shepherd's bag with a few stones in it, and a sling to defend the sheep in case a beast threatened them. With his sling, David could aim and throw a stone as hard and fast as an arrow.

One day, as David led his sheep up a hillside, a lion pounced on a helpless lamb. The flock scattered and their terrified bleating echoed through the mountains. But David faced the lion and struck him with his staff. Stunned, the lion roared in pain.

With another bold stroke, David killed the dreadful lion.

On another day, a bear bounded among the sheep, his teeth bared and his claws ready to attack. Quickly, David put a stone in his sling and flung it at the bear. The creature fell dead at David's feet.

David did not boast of his courage. He believed that his strength came from God. In the mountains, walking through fields of wildflowers and sleeping under the stars, David felt close to the spirit of the Lord.

Alone with the sheep, surrounded by the beauty of nature and the spirit of God, David played his harp. No one in all of Israel played the harp more sweetly. His

songs were tender melodies and the words he sang were songs of praise for the Lord that came from his heart.

At this time, the King of Israel was Saul, a man God had chosen. But Saul had disobeyed the Lord, and in His anger, God sent an evil spirit that troubled the

King. Sometimes Saul felt as if he were enclosed in a black cloud and he suffered terribly.

Saul's attendants worried about their King and, at last, thought of something to help him.

"There is a boy in the mountains," they said, "who plays music so sweet that even the birds stop to listen. Surely his gentle melodies will ease your mind."

And so David was brought to Saul. The King found him pleasing and his music soothing and comforting. He grew fond of the boy and made him his armor bearer, a great honor. Whenever Saul felt his heart grow heavy with sadness, he called for David.

David's soft and calming music so lifted the King's spirits that, after a time, he was well. So Saul sent David back to his father in Bethlehem, knowing that the boy would return whenever he needed him. David went home filled with joy, for he had served his King well.

All during the days that Saul was King, Israel was at war with the Philistines. Finally, the enemy gathered a fierce army on a mountainside overlooking a valley called Elah. Saul sent for men from all of Israel and they came willingly. They pitched their tents on the opposite side of the valley and prepared for the battle that would take place below.

No one expected what happened next.

No army came out of the camp of the Philistines. Only one man strode into the valley. And he was a giant. His name was Goliath of Gath, and he was more than nine feet tall. An enormous helmet covered his head. A long coat of armor hid his body. Large brass plates protected his shoulders and legs. A towering spear was clasped in his hand. The giant shouted to the men of Israel in a voice like thunder. "I am a Philistine and you are servants of Saul! Choose one man and let him come down to me. There is no need for battle. I am only one man, and I ask for only one man."

True, he was only one man. But he was a giant. The men of Israel were afraid.

Twice a day, morning and evening, Goliath came down into the valley and roared his challenge.

"Give me a man to fight," he bellowed. "If he kills me,

then we will be your servants. If I kill him, you will be our servants."

The men of Israel watched the giant and listened to the thunder of his voice and their courage left them.

Every day for forty days, Goliath of Gath dared someone to face him. And every day King Saul and all his soldiers trembled with fear.

Now, David, at the time, was at home in Bethlehem, tending his sheep. But three of his older brothers were in Saul's army. His father, Jesse, sent him to the camp with food for his brothers.

Just as David reached them, Goliath stepped out of the Philistine camp and his voice boomed across the valley.

"Give me a man that we may fight!" he thundered.

David saw the men of Israel turn pale with fear. "Who is this man that challenges the armies of God?" David asked.

"Goliath of Gath," a soldier told him. "Saul promises great riches—and even the hand of his daughter in marriage, to the man who will fight him. But who would dare to fight the giant?"

"I will fight this enemy of God's people," David answered.

David's brother, Eliab, was angry and ashamed, for he thought David was boasting like a foolish boy.

"Go home and tend the sheep," he scolded.

But other men took David seriously and repeated his words to Saul, who sent for the boy. David bowed before the King.

"Let no man's heart tremble because of Goliath," David said. "I, your servant, will fight this Philistine."

"You, fight the giant? You are still a youth, and he is a man of war," Saul said. He gazed at the young man affectionately, for he remembered how David's gentle music had soothed his troubled heart.

"It is true that I am young," David said. "But I have kept my father's sheep. And when the lion and the bear have come to take lambs, I have killed them with my own hands. My strength and courage come from the Lord. He delivered me from the paw of the lion and the paw of the bear, and he will deliver me from the hand of this Philistine."

Saul gazed at David. At last, he said, "Go, and the Lord go with you."

Then the King gave him his own armor. But when David put on the brass helmet, coat of mail, and heavy sword, he could barely walk.

"I am only a shepherd," he said to Saul as he took off the armor. "I must fight in my own way."

So David took his wooden staff, chose five smooth stones from a nearby brook, and put them in his shepherd's bag. Then, with his bag over his shoulder and his sling in his hand, David walked down the mountain slope to meet the giant Goliath.

Goliath strode forward and sneered at what the men of Israel had sent him—a boy with a wooden staff. "Am I a dog, that you come after me with a stick?" he bellowed. "Come, then, and I will feed your flesh to the birds of the air and the beasts of the field."

There was still some distance between them. David walked calmly toward the giant and answered him, for he wanted to be closer.

"You come with a sword and a spear and a shield," the boy called. "But I come in the name of the Lord, the God of the armies of Israel. The Lord will deliver you into our hands."

The giant howled with rage and rushed forward to strike David with his sword. Running toward him, David reached into his shepherd's bag. Quickly, he placed a stone

in his sling. Then he raised his arm, took aim, and threw it with all his strength. The stone flew out of the sling. As swift as an arrow, it struck Goliath right between the eyes. Goliath stopped still and swayed like a great tree. Then the mighty giant toppled as if an ax had cut him to the ground.

The Philistines stared in horror. The men of Israel gasped as they saw the giant that had terrorized them for forty days fall at the hand of a boy with a sling. Surely, they thought, they had seen a miracle.

David ran up to the fallen body. He took Goliath's sword, raised it, and using all his force, killed the giant.

When the Philistines saw that their champion was dead, they scattered in horror. A cheer of rejoicing went up from the army of Israel, and the soldiers plunged after their enemy.

It was a great victory for the forces of Saul.

Throughout Israel David's name was known, and people sang songs of praise to the shepherd who killed the giant in the name of the Lord.

DANIEL AND THE LIONS' DEN

When Daniel was a boy, his home, the holy city of Jerusalem, was destroyed by the Babylonians. At the moment Daniel's city collapsed into ruins, his life as a servant of God began.

Nebuchadnezzar, King of the Babylonians, wished to have some of the young captives from Jerusalem to serve him. He ordered his captain to search for prisoners that were healthy and intelligent. Daniel was one of those chosen. Although Daniel was treated well, he remained faithful to the one true God, and God gave him an understanding of dreams and visions.

Now it happened that some time later Nebuchadnezzar had a dream

44

that troubled him deeply. But he could not remember the dream. He called upon all the wise men in the land, but no one could help him. How could they if he could not tell them the dream?

Yet rage overcame Nebuchadnezzar, and he commanded: "Give me an answer, or every wise man in this land shall die!"

Now Daniel was a wise man, so he was in danger. He prayed to God for the answer, and God revealed the King's dream to him.

Daniel went quickly to the King and said, "The God of my fathers has made your dream known to me. You dreamed of a great image with a head of gold, arms of silver, thighs of brass, and feet of iron and clay. As you watched, a giant stone rolled against the feet and the whole image shattered."

The King listened intently. "Yes!" he said in amazement. "And the meaning?"

"You are the head of gold," Daniel told him, "ruler of the greatest kingdom on earth. But after you, there will be lesser kings, until at last the kingdom is destroyed."

Nebuchadnezzar said, "Your God is God of gods and Lord of Kings, for this is indeed my dream."

From that day on, Daniel remained in the King's court as a trusted servant.

When Nebuchadnezzar died, his son Belshazzar became King, but he was a foolish man who thought only of his own pleasures and not of his country. Nebuchadnezzar's dream came true, for his son was a lesser king. He did not even prepare to fight when the mighty armies of the Medes and Persians threatened his borders.

When his enemies attacked, the kingdom was destroyed, and Darius the Mede took Belshazzar's throne.

Darius had heard about Daniel, his wisdom, and his ability to tell the meaning of dreams. As the new King, Darius chose 120 princes to rule the kingdom with three presidents above them. He made Daniel the first president. Daniel accepted, believing that God planned it so.

The task was not easy. The other princes and presidents were jealous of Daniel and tried to find fault with him. But they could not. So they plotted against him.

They had noticed that Daniel went into his house three times a day to pray. He stood before a window facing the ruined city of Jerusalem and chanted his prayers.

These jealous men found a way to use Daniel's prayers against him. They approached the King. "O mighty King," they said, "we have prepared a new law to honor you. This law will say that for thirty days no one may pray to any god or man, except the King. Anyone who breaks this law shall be thrown into a den of lions."

Darius was flattered, and he signed his name.

Now Daniel knew of the law, but he continued to pray three times a day. The jealous princes saw him at his window and heard him praying to his God. At once they hurried off to Darius.

"Is it not true, O King," they said, "that no law of the Medes or the Persians can be changed?"

"That is true," Darius answered.

"Then Daniel must be thrown into the lions' den," they told him, "for three times a day he prays to a god other than you."

Darius knew then that he had been tricked. He had not thought of Daniel when he signed that law. He tried to think of some way to save Daniel. But the stern law of the Medes and the Persians left no escape. Reluctantly, Darius sent for Daniel and commanded that he be thrown into a den of lions.

Darius went to the mouth of the pit where Daniel had been taken. He saw Daniel standing fearlessly among the lions, and he called down to him, "May the God you serve deliver you from death." Then sadly, the King turned away, and a great stone was rolled over the mouth of the pit.

King Darius spent a restless night. His every thought was with Daniel, left in darkness among the ferocious lions. Early in the morning, he rushed to the den, dreading what he would find. "Daniel!" he cried out.

Daniel's voice answered from the lions' den. "O King! God sent His angel to shut the lions' mouths. I am not hurt. I am innocent in the sight of the Lord. And I am innocent before you. I have done no wrong!"

The King rejoiced. He ordered his guards to take Daniel from the lions' den, and they looked with awe upon the living Daniel, saved by his Lord.

JONAH AND THE WHALE

Jonah was a prophet of the Lord in the land of Israel. God spoke to him and gave him messages to bring to the people. His task was to go wherever God sent him and say whatever God told him. A prophet could not choose for himself or disobey the Lord.

But once, Jonah disobeyed.

"Go to Nineveh, that great city in Assyria," God commanded him. "The people there are behaving in evil ways." The Lord wanted His teachings spread to the people of other lands, for they were His children, too.

But Jonah was an Israelite and cared little for the people of Nineveh. "They are worshipping idols and becoming more wicked every year," he thought. "Why should they not suffer for their sins? Why should I rescue them by teaching them to worship the one true God?"

Jonah decided not to go. Instead he went to the seaport of Joppa and boarded a ship going to Tarshish, which was in the opposite direction and very far away.

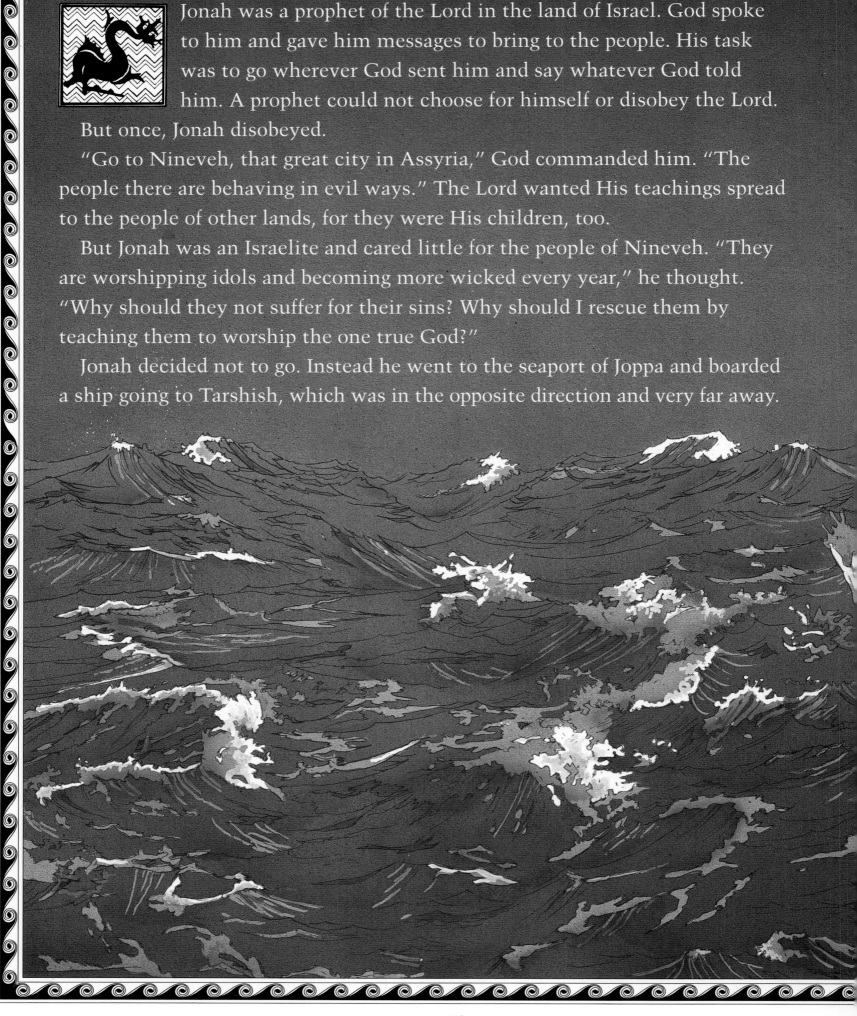

"Surely," he thought, "the Lord will not be looking for me there."

But it is not possible to escape the presence of the Lord. He knew where Jonah was and He knew what was in His prophet's heart.

When the ship sailed, Jonah went below the deck to rest. When the wind rose, he did not hear it, for he was asleep. When the waves swelled and rocked the boat, he did not feel it, for he still slept.

The Lord made the wind blow harder. The waves became huge and lashed the boat. The decks were flooded with furious water. The ship's wooden timbers trembled.

The sailors were terrified, for they had never seen such a dreadful storm. Each one prayed desperately to whatever god he believed in. "Calm the seas!" they pleaded. But none of their gods could deliver them from the storm.

The captain of the ship went down to Jonah. "Wake up!" he cried. "How can you sleep? Pray to your god so that he may keep us from dying."

Jonah came on deck, but he did not pray. How could he ask anything from God when he was fleeing from Him? The storm raged on. The wind howled, and the boat shook as if it would fly into pieces.

The sailors turned to Jonah. "I am the cause of this awful punishment," he said. "Blame me."

Alarmed, they questioned him. "Where do you come from?" they demanded. "What do you do?"

"I am a Hebrew from the land of Israel," Jonah said, "and I serve the Lord, the God of Heaven, who made the sea and the dry land." And he told the men the truth about why he was aboard their ship.

When the sailors heard that Jonah had fled the presence of the Lord, they were afraid. "Why have you done this to us?" they cried angrily. "What can we do?"

"You must throw me into the sea," Jonah replied, "for only then will the wind stop."

But the sailors were good men and did not

want to throw Jonah overboard. In a panic, they prayed to the Lord of Israel. "We are innocent," they cried. "Do not let us die for the sake of punishing this one man." But the storm was more violent than before.

Finally, Jonah insisted that they cast him into the sea. They lifted him and threw him over the side into the raging water. Jonah disappeared in the whirling ocean. The wind softened to a breeze, and the waves fell to a gentle roll. The sea became calm.

Now the Lord had prepared a great fish to swallow Jonah when he fell into the water. The huge fish swallowed him without a bite. Swirled and tumbled, Jonah was horrified to find himself in the belly of the fish. He had expected death, but not this! The inside of a fish! How dark and wet it was! How cold and smelly!

Jonah moaned miserably and prayed, hoping that the Lord would hear him.

After three days and three nights, God spoke to the fish. It opened its enormous mouth, lifted its giant head, and spit Jonah out onto dry land. Drenched, coughing and gasping, Jonah lay on the beach. As soon as his breath returned, Jonah thanked God for delivering him.

Jonah rested, and then he journeyed to Nineveh as the Lord had commanded him in the beginning. He preached to the people about changing their evil ways, and they did.

And so Jonah, the prophet, brought the Word of God into another land and served his
Lord well.